The Kuklapolitan Players Present

The Dragon Who Lived Downstairs

by Burr Tillstrom
illustrated by David Small

FEATURING THE KUKLAPOLITAN CHARACTERS CREATED BY BURR TILLSTROM

William Morrow and Company • New York 1984

1 2 3 4 5 6 7 8 9 10

Library of Congress Cataloging in Publication Data
Tillstrom, Burr.   The dragon who lived downstairs.
Summary: An impoverished princess and her mother are aided by a kindly dragon in vanquishing a wicked
witch who wants to steal their castle's gold. [1. Fairy tales] I. Small, David, 1945-   ill.
II. Title. PZ8.T485Dr 1983   [E]   83-17285
ISBN 0-688-02734-2
ISBN 0-688-02735-0 (lib. bdg.)

To my dear friends, Fran and Eda

Once upon a time, in a kingdom far away, there lived a king and a queen and their little daughter, Princess Mildred. As kingdoms go, theirs was a small and rather poor one, for although both the king and queen were royal, they had very little money. This was a source of great irritation to the queen, who came from a long line of royalty. As a matter of fact, upon the slightest provocation, she would tell you how she was the second daughter of the second daughter of a king who, in turn, was the second son of the second daughter of a king, and so on as far back as anyone could remember.

Her husband, the king, was also very royal, but didn't talk about it much. He was content to work in the garden with his prize geraniums or to do odd jobs around the castle . . . like tuck-pointing.

This sort of thing infuriated the queen, who felt that Mildred should be brought up in the very best surroundings—particularly since she was a *first* daughter and someday would be queen herself. The queen was forever after the king to go out and conquer another kingdom or search for buried treasure—she had heard there was such a treasure in a castle across the mountains—so they could be rich as well as royal.

After one especially trying day of paying the bills, the
queen grew very exasperated and said to the king:

"Your Majesty!"

"Yes, ma'am," said the king, without looking up from a
lovely yellow geranium he was transplanting.

"I can't bear this another moment. Mildred's clothes are
in tatters. My ermine robe has moths and the diamonds in
your crown have all been sold. If you don't go and find
that treasure immediately, I shall go home to Mother and
take the princess with me."

The king was loath to give up his pleasant ways. But he realized that life was no longer just a bed of geraniums. And so he polished his sword, kissed his wife and little Mildred good-bye, put on his helmet, and headed for the castle on the other side of the mountains.

The days turned into weeks, the weeks into months, and the months into years, and still the king did not return. The queen, who was really not a bad woman— just too proud—was very sad and wept copiously every time she remembered how she had sent her husband away.

"Oh, if I could just see him coming across the drawbridge," she sighed. "He could putter around with his old geraniums or anything. We'd get along somehow."

The little Princess Mildred missed her father very much, but after all, she was only a child when he left and there were many things to occupy her time. She had a wonderful friend who lived in the kingdom next door—a handsome young fellow named Edgar, who was very rich but not very royal.

They spent many hours together fishing in the river, climbing trees, and picking wild flowers in the meadow. As a matter of fact, as they grew older they fell very much in love and would have married, but the queen was still too proud. Edgar might be rich, but he was not royal enough.

It wasn't long before their castle fell into disrepair. It needed tuck-pointing, and all the geraniums had long since been crowded out by weeds. The queen did everything she could to make ends meet, but on the princess's sixteenth birthday, when the mortgage came due, she realized they would have to give up the old homestead. Sadly, she told her daughter that they would have to leave the castle.

"But, Mother," said Mildred, "why can't I marry Edgar? He's rich, and besides, I love him."

"But he isn't royal. Remember your position, Mildred dear. One day you shall be queen and you must marry a crown prince or at least a second son. Come along and pack."

The princess was brokenhearted at the thought of leaving Edgar, but she was a good daughter and would not forsake her mother. As the princess and her beloved parted, she gave him her little jeweled mirror as a keepsake.

"I shall never part with it," Edgar promised. "And don't weep, little princess. Soon I shall be a knight and my first quest will be to find you."

And so the queen and the princess started off for their new home—a rented castle some distance off—that the queen had heard of through her cook. It was a rather rundown place without modern conveniences, but roomy and old-fashioned and very cheap, so the cook said.

The trip took many days. Side by side they trudged through forests, over streams, and across the mountains. The queen pretended it was a royal camping trip, and the spirits of the princess were quite high as she thought of her lover, who would soon follow them.

At last they arrived at the castle. It was large and rather gloomy on the outside, and very dusty inside.

"Well, my dear, here we are," said the queen, "our new home. It's not what I would have wished for you." She pushed aside a cobweb. "I don't know how we'll manage to clean it up without servants."

"Don't worry, Mother," said the princess, "I'll help. You take the upstairs and I'll take the downstairs."

So the queen tied a handkerchief around her hair and went upstairs to hang pictures. "It's more like home when the pictures are up," she always said. The princess went around busily dusting off some of the old furniture downstairs (for it was a furnished castle) and she was just dusting off a table when she heard a knock.

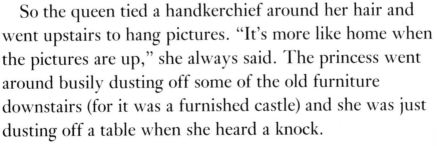

"Someone calling so soon?" she said to herself. "I wonder who it can be."

She went to the front door, but no one was there. "I must have been hearing things," she said, and went back to her dusting. Then it came again—a sharper knock this time.

"Well, it must be the back door," she said to herself, and went out through the kitchen. But when she opened the door, there was no one there either.

"Maybe this castle is haunted," she said. "Maybe that's why it was so cheap. Oh well, one can get used to anything, I guess." And so she took up her dusting again. Then the knock came again, louder than ever.

"It seems to be coming from downstairs," Mildred said. "I do believe someone is knocking on the basement ceiling."

She looked under the rug and lo and behold, there was a trapdoor. She grasped the great iron ring, and pulling with all her might, she opened the trapdoor and . . .

. . . up popped a dragon.

"Hello," said the dragon. "Are you my new neighbor? I live downstairs."

"Well, hello," said the princess. "My name is Mildred. I am a princess and we just moved in."

"Oh, how do you do, Your Highness. My name is Dorchester Dragon."

"How do you do, Mr. Dragon."

"Oh, please call me Dorchester, Your Highness."

"Then you must call me Mildred," said the princess.

"Mildred—that's a lovely name," said the dragon. "I'm very happy you moved in. I've been very lonely here all by myself."

"I didn't think anyone else lived here," she said. "I mean—do you own this castle or are you renting, too, Dorchester?"

"Heavens, no! I work here. I tend the fire and rake the leaves and cut the grass." He paused. "Did your whole family come with you?"

"Oh, no . . . just my mother, and she doesn't like me to talk to strangers."

The dragon looked a little downcast at this and the Princess hastened to add, "But you aren't a stranger, Dorchester; you're a neighbor! I'm awfully glad you live downstairs. I was afraid I would be lonely here, but perhaps you'll come up for tea. And if you care to borrow anything, like a cup of sugar, please feel free."

"Well, thank you, Mildred. That's real neighborly of you. And you must come and visit me sometime."

"I'd love to," said Mildred, looking into the basement. "What's that shining down there?"

"Oh, that's the gold."

"The gold? What gold?"

Just then they heard the queen call from upstairs. "Mildred! Who are you talking to down there?"

"We'll continue this later," said Dorchester. "I think it best if I meet your mother gradually. Some people are a little startled to come across me all at once." And he popped back down into the cellar, pulling the trapdoor closed after him.

"Mildred, dear, did you bring your mirror?" asked the queen. "There isn't a single mirror in this whole castle."

"No, I didn't, Mother. But, Mother," she went on excitedly, "guess what?"

"What, darling?" said the queen. "I do wish we had remembered to pack a mirror. How am I ever going to comb my hair?"

"I've just been talking to a dragon," said the princess.

"Oh, that's nice, darling," said the queen. "Now bring me the hammer and nails so that we can hang these pictures upstairs. A—what—?"

"A dragon, Mother—a real dragon. He lives downstairs."

"Mildred, are you feeling well?"

"I feel wonderful, Mother, and I'm ever so much happier. He's a nice dragon."

"Now, Mildred, you're too old for this kind of fairy tale. If you don't feel well, Mama will give you some hot

milk and put you to bed. But if you're indulging your
imagination again, you can just stop it. There's work
to be done and there's no time for make-believe."

"But, Mother, this isn't make-believe. He lives
downstairs. Right here. Look!" Mildred pulled open
the trapdoor, but the queen had already gone.
"Mr. Dragon, Mr. Dragon . . . Dorchester!"

"She's gone, Dorchester."

"She didn't believe you, did she? They never do."

"Tell me again about the gold," said the princess.

"I'm guarding it."

"Guarding it for who?"

"I don't rightly remember. All I know is I'm supposed to guard it. My father guarded it before me, and his father before him. And I don't mind admitting it gets pretty dull around here. But it's my job and I do it the best I know how."

"Why don't you give the gold away? Then you could leave."

"Who would I give it to? The witch enchants everyone."

"What witch?" said Mildred, looking around in alarm.

"Don't worry. Nothing will happen to you, Princess, as long as I'm around."

"Mildred—Mildred," came a voice from the stairs.

"There's your mother again," said Dorchester.

"Mildred! Get away from that nasty hole!" screamed the queen. "Heaven alone knows what's down there."

And just at that moment the dragon reappeared. With a shriek, the queen fell over backward, knocking her crown clear across the room.

"Mildred, run for your life, dear! Mother will save you from this horrible snake!"

"I'm not a snake, ma'am. I am a dragon."

The queen gasped. "I can't believe my eyes!"

"You see, Mother? It's true. This is our neighbor, Mr. Dorchester Dragon. This is my mother, Dorchester. She's a queen."

"Pleased to know you, ma'am."

The queen nodded icily. "Only my friends call me ma'am. When addressing me, please call me Your Majesty."

"Yes, My Majesty," said the dragon humbly.

"What you are doing in our castle? I understood there was no one else living here."

"But I told you, Mother . . . he's the caretaker. He tends the fire and rakes the leaves and cuts the grass and guards the gold."

"I don't care what he does! I'll not have the janitor coming upstairs cluttering up our dining room."

"But he's our neighbor, Mother, and I told him he could come up for tea or to borrow a cup of sugar."

"That's the way these things start— first a cup of sugar, then a pound of flour, and then they've moved into your apartment. Nosirree! You go back down where you belong and stay there."

"But, Mother, he guards the gold. . . ."

"I don't care what he does. I want him out of here now."

"But, My Majesty, I was only trying to warn you about the wicked witch. You see, I'm the only one she's afraid of. She's after the gold in the basement and she works spells and enchants everyone who comes to this castle."

"Spells? Enchantments?" said the queen, taking a sudden interest. "Are you by any chance under an enchantment? Are you really a royal prince?"

"Oh, no, ma'am—My Majesty. I am a dragon. My father was a dragon before me and his father before him. We've been dragons as far back as anyone can remember."

"Then down you go!" With that, the queen gave him a great push, and he fell back into the cellar.

"But, Mother," cried the princess.

"I don't care. I will not have a dragon in my house." And while the princess wept, the queen closed the trapdoor, nailed it tight to the floor and, for good measure, pulled the heavy dining-room table over it.

At that moment a knock came at the kitchen door.

"Oh, heavens, child, it's the neighbors calling. Now dry your eyes and remember, we are royal."

The queen opened the kitchen door and there stood a sweet little old lady with a pocketbook over one arm and a basket over the other.

"How do, little girl, is the lady of the house at home?" said the old woman.

This caught the queen quite off guard and in spite of her recent annoyance, she smiled. "Why . . . I'm the lady of the house and this is my daughter, Princess Mildred."

"Princess? Then you must be a queen—Your Majesty."

"You may call me ma'am."

"Thank you, Mrs. Ma'am. And this is your daughter?" said the old lady. "Heavens to Betsy! I can't believe it. You seem more like sisters."

"Oh, now, really," said the queen, pleased with the flattery. "But thank you anyway. What may we do for you, my dear?"

"Oh, I just have a few little things I thought you might want to buy—shoelaces, thread, and some lovely homemade gingerbread."

"Mama," said the princess, "I don't like her."

"Hush, child," replied her mother. "Remember your manners. She's just a poor old soul trying to earn a living." She opened the door wider. "Won't you come in, my dear?"

"Well, I don't know. . . ." said the old lady.

"Oh, don't let my appearance frighten you," said the queen. "I've just had a terrible set-to with a dragon who lives downstairs."

"'Bye."

"Oh, don't worry. I took care of him," said the queen. "I pushed him down in the basement and nailed the trapdoor shut."

"Oooh, you did? Real tight?"

"Yes, real tight."

"Well, then, in that case, I'd be happy to sit for a spell. You see, I'm allergic to dragons."

The old lady stepped across the threshold, then quickly she slammed the door behind her and locked it tight.

"Aha," she cried. "Just what I've been waiting for. That dragon is the only creature I'm afraid of and now you've locked him up. Thank you, you've done me a great favor. I'm not a poor old lady at all; I'm a wicked witch, and I've come for the gold that's hidden in the castle."

"Gold!" said the queen, looking at Mildred. "I thought you said 'coal.'"

Wasting no time, the witch continued, "I'm going to enchant you both so you can't get in my way as I search for the gold. Now, let's see. . . . I think I shall turn the princess into a spool of yellow thread."

And in a twinkling and a puff of smoke, the princess was a spool of yellow thread. Peering at the queen, the witch said, "But what will I do with you, plump one?"

"I can't believe my eyes," the queen gasped.

"The eyes have it!" cried the witch. And in another twinkling and a puff of smoke, the queen was turned into a package of needles.

Chuckling gleefully, the old witch tucked them both into her basket with the shoelaces and gingerbread and started on her search for the gold.

She rummaged through the window seats, the kitchen cabinets, and the queen's trunk, but she couldn't find the gold because, as we know, it was downstairs in the cellar. Finally, she said to herself, "It must be down in the cellar. And wouldn't you know, that dragon is still down there! How can I get the gold?"

Just then, she heard the clatter of horse hooves. She looked out of the window and there, riding toward the castle, was a young knight. (It was our Edgar, of course.) Swiftly he rode across the drawbridge and knocked at the castle door.

"Mildred," he called out. "Princess Mildred, are you there?"

"Hee, hee, hee, hee," the witch chuckled gleefully. "I have a plan. I'll get this knight to slay the dragon and I'll get the gold and maybe marry him to boot."

Quick as a wink, the witch dressed herself in one of the princess's gowns. Seizing an old wig that had fallen out of the queen's trunk, she clamped it on her head and rushed down to open the door.

"Oh, you've come to save me! You've come to save me, my brave and handsome knight!" she cried.

Edgar looked startled. "But you're not the princess Mildred."

"Oh, yes," said the witch.

"But the princess Mildred is beautiful and young."

"Well, time flies, sweetie pie, and besides, I'm enchanted by a wicked old dragon that lives in the basement."

"A dragon?" said Edgar.

"Oh, yes. A most ferocious dragon! When we came to the castle, he leaped upon us and ate up Mother and put a spell on me. If you would only slay him!"

"Oh, Mildred, my love," cried Edgar. "I will save you." He pulled his shining sword from its scabbard and charged into the castle. "Where is this dragon? Show him to me and I will slay him."

"Follow me," said the witch and she led him into the dining room. "See, I've nailed fast the trapdoor."

Working feverishly, they moved the table and pulled out the nails.

"Now, when I pull it open, rush the dragon immediately," said the witch. "Don't wait, slay him at once. Otherwise, he'll gobble you up or enchant you. Don't listen to a word he says. Are you ready?"

"Ready, my princess," cried Edgar.

"All rightee now, on the count of three. One . . . two . . . three. . . ."

With a mighty tug, she pulled open the trapdoor and then ran behind the drapery as the dragon popped into view. With sword in hand, Edgar charged.

"Stop," said the dragon, "I'm your friend."

Edgar hesitated.

"Don't listen to him!" screamed the witch. But it was too late. Edgar had waited too long.

Dorchester knocked the sword out of Edgar's hand and seized him by the nose.

"Don't listen to her. She's a witch, she's a witch," warned Dorchester.

"Don't talk with your mouth full," cried Edgar. "Can't you fight like a gentleman?"

"I don't want to fight you," said the dragon, letting go. "I want to save you. The witch enchanted the princess and the queen. I'm the only one who can stop her."

The witch was beside herself with fury and leaped from her hiding place. "Do as I say! Do as I say, or I'll enchant you."

"Oh, ho," said Edgar, "then it's true. You are a witch."

"Yes, yes, it's true, but it's too late. I'm going to turn you into a pin cushion."

"Quick, have you a mirror?" asked the dragon.

"Yes, I always carry the little jeweled mirror that Mildred gave to me," said Edgar.

"Then hold it up, quickly," cried the dragon.

The witch approached Edgar, mumbling magical words. Edgar desperately searched through his pockets and just as the witch finished her spell, he held the mirror up in front of her, not quite knowing what to expect.

There was a moment of absolute silence as the witch caught sight of herself and then it happened: She started to laugh. "Hee, hee, hee, hee, hee, hee."

Louder and louder her laugh rang through the castle.

"If that isn't the funniest thing I've ever seen! What a face! Hoo, hoo, hoo, hoo, hee, hee, hoo, hoo."

With hardly a pause to catch her breath, she grabbed the mirror from Edgar's hand and ran out of the castle, still laughing hysterically.

"What happened?" said Edgar. "I don't understand."

"It's simple," said the dragon. "She's laughing at herself. If you can laugh at yourself, you can never be very wicked."

No sooner had the dragon spoken than they both heard another laugh. It was the merry laugh of Princess Mildred. The enchantment was broken!

"My beloved," cried Edgar.

"My neighbor," cried the dragon.

"My handsome knight," cried the princess as she flew to Edgar's arms.

"My husband," cried the queen as she and the king suddenly appeared. "I can't believe my eyes."

"Yes, my dear, I was a shoelace," said the king. "The wicked witch enchanted me, too, when I came to get the gold."

Then the queen apologized, first to the dragon and then to Edgar. And to Mildred she said humbly, "It doesn't matter about royalty."

"You're right, my dear," the king agreed. "Mildred, we give our consent. You and Edgar can be married at once."

And so they all settled down in the big, old castle which, of course, they were able to buy with the gold in the basement, and since it was old-fashioned and roomy, they remodeled it into a two-family affair. They also remodeled the basement into a very snug apartment, complete with shower stall, and Dorchester Dragon stayed on forever and ever. And they even put in an oil burner so he didn't have to tend the fire anymore.

As for the witch, no one has heard of her since. But if someday there comes a gentle knock and you open the door to find a sweet little old lady with a pocketbook over one arm and a basket in the other, don't invite her in—unless you have a mirror handy.